Sports Illustrated KIDS

Sports Illustrated Kids: Legend vs. Legend

DEREK JETER VS. ALEX RODRIGUEZ

BASEBALL LEGENDS FACE OFF

by Brendan Flynn

CAPSTONE PRESS
a capstone imprint

Published by Capstone Press, an imprint of Capstone
1710 Roe Crest Drive, North Mankato, Minnesota 56003
capstonepub.com

Library of Congress Cataloging-in-Publication Data
Names: Flynn, Brendan, 1968– author.
Title: Derek Jeter vs. Alex Rodriguez : baseball legends face off / by Brendan Flynn.
Description: North Mankato, Minnesota : Capstone Press, [2025] | Series: Sports illustrated kids: legend vs. legend | Includes bibliographical references and index. | Audience: Ages 9–11 Audience: Grades 4–6 | Summary: "Derek Jeter and Alex Rodriguez are baseball superstars! Between the two, Jeter has won more World Series titles, but Rodriguez was a better home run hitter. So which one is the all-time best? Young readers can decide for themselves by comparing the fantastic feats and stunning stats of two legendary pro baseball players"— Provided by publisher.
Identifiers: LCCN 2024017443 (print) | LCCN 2024017444 (ebook) | ISBN 9781669089445 (hardcover) | ISBN 9781669089674 (paperback) | ISBN 9781669089483 (pdf) ISBN 9781669089698 (kindle edition) | ISBN 9781669089681 (epub)
Subjects: LCSH: Baseball players—United States—Rating of—Juvenile literature. | Jeter, Derek, 1974– Juvenile literature. | Rodriguez, Alex, 1975– Juvenile literature. | Baseball players—United States--Biography—Juvenile literature. | Shortstop (Baseball)—United States—Juvenile literature.
Classification: LCC GV865.A1 F57 2025 (print) | LCC GV865.A1 (ebook) | DDC 796.3570922 [B]—dc23/eng/20240427
LC record available at https://lccn.loc.gov/2024017443
LC ebook record available at https://lccn.loc.gov/2024017444

Editorial Credits
Editor: Ericka Smith; Designer: Tracy Davies; Media Researcher: Svetlana Zhurkin; Production Specialist: Whitney Schaefer

Image Credits
Associated Press: Bill Kostroun, 20; Getty Images: Adam Glanzman, 6, Adam Hunger, 17, Al Bello, 13, Alex Goodlett, 11, Allsport/Brian Bahr, 7, Brian Bahr, 21, 22, Christian Petersen, 5, Christopher Pasatieri, 12, Dilip Vishwanat, 23, Elsa, 9, 15, J. Meric, 18, Jed Jacobsohn, 24, 25, Jim McIsaac, 19, 28, Lisa Blumenfeld, cover (right), Mike Stobe, 14, MLB/Rich Pilling, 27, Otto Greule Jr, cover (left), 29, Rob Carr, 10, Sports Imagery/John Capella, 26, Stephen Dunn, 4, The Boston Globe/Barry Chin, 16; Shutterstock: saicle (background), cover and throughout; Sports Illustrated: Walter Iooss Jr., 8

Printed in the United States 6758

CONTENTS

** * * All stats current through the 2023 season. * * **

Words in **bold** appear in the glossary.

Baseball Legends Face Off!

Derek Jeter and Alex Rodriguez were baseball superstars. They thrilled fans with big hits and **clutch** defensive plays. Jeter was famous for his consistency. Rodriguez (A-Rod) was known as a power hitter.

But which player is the best? Let's find out!

Derek Jeter

Alex Rodriguez

THE MATCHUP	Born	City
Jeter	June 26, 1974	Pequannock, New Jersey
Rodriguez	July 27, 1975	New York, New York

Height and Weight

Baseball players don't have to be big to play well. But A-Rod and Jeter were big guys! Rodriguez and Jeter were the same height. But Rodriguez weighed about 35 pounds (15.9 kilograms) more than Jeter. That extra muscle helped Rodriguez hit the ball far. But Jeter's slim build helped him chase down balls at **shortstop**.

Rodriguez at bat during a 2016 game against the Boston Red Sox

Jeter chasing a ball during a 2001 World Series game

THE MATCHUP	Height	Weight
Rodriguez	6 feet, 3 inches (191 centimeters)	230 pounds (104.3 kg)
Jeter	6 feet, 3 inches	195 pounds (88.5 kg)

Games Played

A-Rod played 22 seasons and 2,784 games. Jeter played 2,747 games during 20 seasons. Both were **dependable**. A season is 162 games long. A-Rod played at least 150 games in nine seasons. Jeter played at least 150 games in 13 seasons.

Rodriguez playing for the Seattle Mariners in 1998

Jeter batting for the New York Yankees in 2014

THE MATCHUP	Seasons Played	Games Played	Season Played 150+ Games	Teams
Rodriguez	22	2,784	9	Seattle Mariners, Texas Rangers, New York Yankees
Jeter	20	2,747	13	New York Yankees

Home Runs

A-Rod was a big home run hitter. He had 696 **career** homers. He hit two homers in 57 games—and three homers in five games. He also hit 25 grand slams!

Jeter wasn't known as a home run hitter. But he hit 260 career homers. He also had 10 two-homer games and one grand slam.

Rodriguez running the bases after hitting a grand slam in 2011

Jeter hitting a home run in 2014

THE MATCHUP	Home Runs	Two-Homer Games	Three-Homer Games	Grand Slams
Rodriguez	696	57	5	25
Jeter	260	10	0	1

Hits

Only 33 players have at least 3,000 career hits in the major leagues. Jeter and Rodriguez are in that club. Jeter had 3,465 career hits. He also had 544 **doubles** and 66 **triples**. A-Rod had 3,115 career hits, 548 doubles, and 31 triples.

Jeter celebrating 3,000 hits in 2011

Rodriguez making his 3,000th career hit in 2015

THE MATCHUP	Hits	Doubles	Triples
Jeter	3,465	544	66
Rodriguez	3,115	548	31

Runs Batted In

Power hitters are counted on to drive in runs. Rodriguez was no exception. A-Rod had 2,086 career runs batted in (RBIs). He was one of the greatest RBI producers of all time! Jeter had just 1,311 career RBIs.

Rodriguez hitting an RBI in a 2011 game

Jeter hitting an RBI in 2014

THE MATCHUP	RBIs
Rodriguez	2,086
Jeter	1,311

Runs Scored

In baseball, scoring runs is the name of the game. Jeter and Rodriguez scored a lot of them! Jeter crossed home plate 1,923 times. Only 10 players have scored more runs. A-Rod had 2,021 career runs. He's eighth on the all-time list.

Jeter sliding into home during an American League Championship Series game

Rodriguez diving toward home plate during a 2015 game

THE MATCHUP	Runs Scored
Jeter	1,923
Rodriguez	2,021

Stolen Bases

A timely stolen base can be key in a big rally. Jeter was a smart base runner. He had 358 career steals. He was caught stealing 97 times. Rodriguez stole 329 bases. He was caught 76 times. A-Rod's success rate of 81.2 percent was slightly better than Jeter's 78.7 percent.

Jeter stealing second base in 2010

Rodriguez making the steal at third base during a 2011 game

THE MATCHUP	Stolen Bases	Caught Stealing	Success Rate
Jeter	358	97	78.7 percent
Rodriguez	329	76	81.2 percent

Fielding

Jeter played shortstop his entire career. His career fielding percentage was .976. He won five **Gold Glove Awards**.

A-Rod began his career as a shortstop for the Mariners. He won two Gold Gloves with the Rangers. His fielding percentage of .973 almost matched Jeter's.

Jeter receiving a Gold Glove in 2005

Rodriguez playing shortstop for the Rangers in 2003

THE MATCHUP	Career Fielding Percentage	Gold Glove Awards
Jeter	.976	5
Rodriguez	.973	2

All-Star Games

The **All-Star Game** (ASG) is played every July. Both A-Rod and Jeter were named to the All-Star team 14 times.

A-Rod played in 11 ASGs. He had seven hits in 26 at-bats and hit one All-Star homer.

Jeter played in 13 ASGs. He had 13 hits in 27 at-bats and also hit one homer.

Rodriguez at bat during the 1998 All-Star Game

Jeter playing in the 2009 All-Star Game

THE MATCHUP	All-Star Nominations	All-Star Games Played	Batting Average	All-Star Home Runs
Rodriguez	14	11	.269	1
Jeter	14	13	.481	1

Postseason

Jeter went to the playoffs 16 times with the Yankees. He played in 158 **postseason** games. He also hit 20 postseason homers. He went to the World Series seven times. And he won five championships.

A-Rod won his only World Series with the Yankees in 2009. Overall, he had 13 homers in just 76 postseason games.

Jeter celebrating a World Series win in 2009

Rodriguez celebrating his only World Series win in 2009

THE MATCHUP	Postseason Games	Postseason Home Runs	World Series Titles
Jeter	158	20	5
Rodriguez	76	13	1

MVP Awards

Each year, the American League (AL) gives an MVP award to the best player in the league. The AL named A-Rod MVP three times.

Jeter never won an AL MVP Award. But in 2000, he was the MVP of the All-Star Game and the World Series.

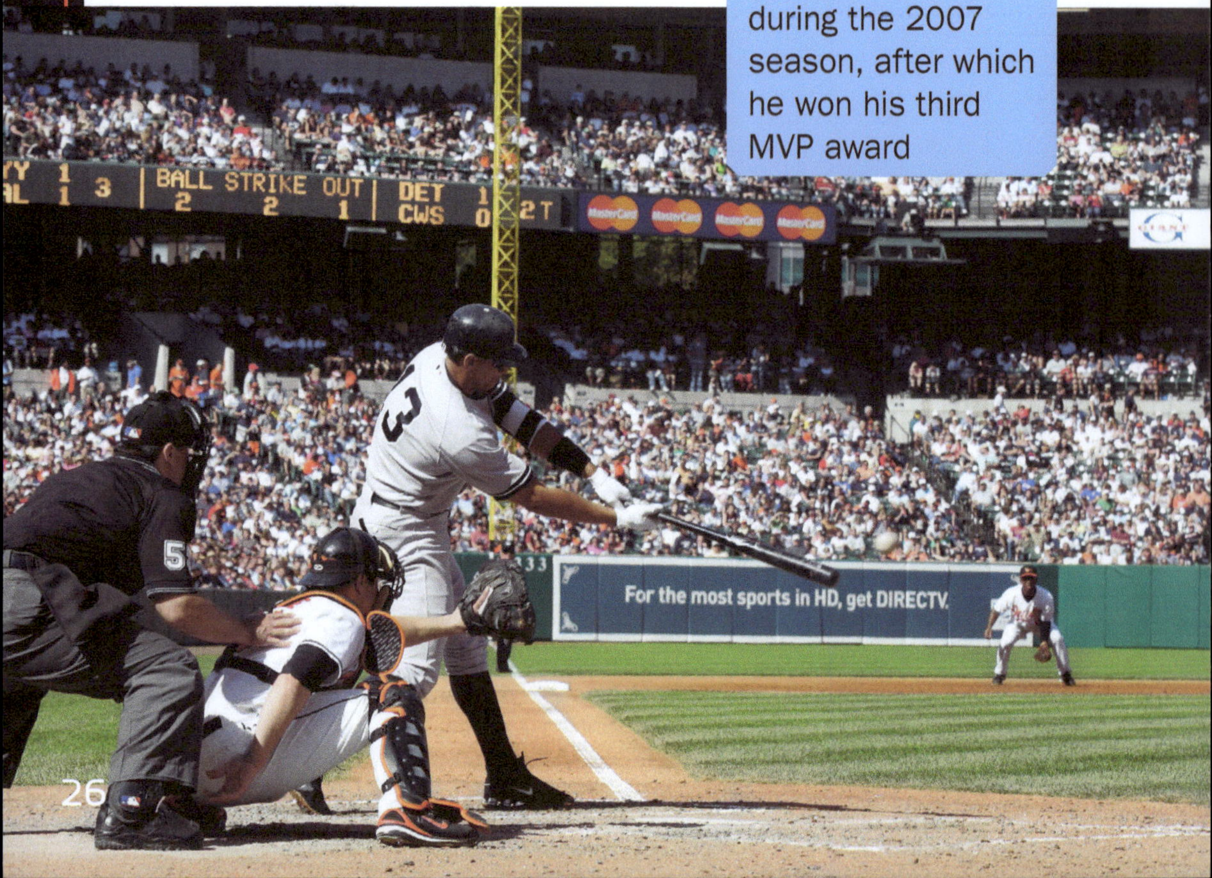

Rodriguez at bat during the 2007 season, after which he won his third MVP award

Jeter with his All-Star Game MVP award in 2000

THE MATCHUP	American League MVP Awards	All-Star Game MVP Awards	World Series MVP Awards
Rodriguez	3	0	0
Jeter	0	1	1

Who Is the Best?

Rodriguez and Jeter are baseball legends. They played the same position for 10 seasons. Then they played alongside each other for 10 more years. A-Rod has the edge in home runs, runs, RBIs, and MVP awards. Jeter has more hits, stolen bases, and World Series titles.

Who is the best player? You make the call!

Rodriguez batting for the Yankees in 2015

Jeter stealing a base during a 2004 game with the Yankees

Glossary

All-Star Game (AWL-star GAYM)—a game held every July featuring the best players in the American League against the best players of the National League

career (kuh-REER)—including everything between a player's first and last game

clutch (KLUHCH)—contributing to a key moment in a game

dependable (duh-PEN-duh-buhl)—can be counted on

double (DUHB-uhl)—a hit that ends with the batter on second base

Gold Glove Award (GOHLD GLUHV uh-WARD)—an award given to the best fielder in each position

postseason (pohst-SEE-zuhn)—the games played after the regular season to determine a champion

shortstop (SHORT-stahp)—a defensive position between second and third base

triple (TRIH-puhl)—a hit that ends with the batter on third base

Read More

Flynn, Brendan. *The MLB Encyclopedia*. Minneapolis: ABDO Publishing Company, 2021.

Smith, Elliott. *Baseball's Greatest Myths and Legends*. North Mankato, MN: Capstone Press, 2023.

Starr, Abbe L. *Derek Jeter: Baseball's Captain*. Minneapolis: Lerner Publications, 2023.

Internet Sites

Major League Baseball
mlb.com

National Baseball Hall of Fame
baseballhall.org

Sports Illustrated Kids: Baseball
sikids.com/baseball

Index

About the Author

Brendan Flynn lives in Minnesota. In addition to writing about sports, Flynn enjoys solving crossword puzzles, trying new recipes in the kitchen, and walking around the beautiful lakes of Minneapolis.